WHEN DEATH
IS
IMMINENT

GREG D. HARDEGREE

S. H. M. Publishing
Abilene, Texas

WHEN DEATH
IS
IMMINENT

Published by:

> S.H.M. Publishing
> P.O. Box 6089 - T
> Abilene, Texas 79608, U.S.A.
> Office / Fax: (915) 692-3223

Cover photograph by: PCA International, Inc., used with permission.
Dedication photograph by: Olan Mills, Inc., used with permission.
Author's photograph by the author.

Publisher's Cataloging in Publication
(Prepared by Quality Books Inc.)

Hardegree, Greg D.
>   When death is imminent / Greg D. Hardegree.
>   p. cm.
>   Preassigned LCCN: 95-69774
>   ISBN: 0-9647177-6-X

>   1. Thanatology. 2. Death. 3. Grief. 4. Family. I. Title

HQ1073.H37 1995   306.88
                                    QBI95-20302

ABOUT THE AUTHOR

Greg Hardegree has been in the medical field for the past eighteen years. He is accustomed to working with terminally ill patients, and is no stranger to death. Like many medical professionals, Greg had become somewhat hardened, or he thought he had, to watching these people pass from this life. It wasn't until he lost his 39 year old wife to cancer that he received a large dose of reality. This caused him to view terminal illness, death, and dying in an entirely different way, and helped him see clearly, the many facets of grief. He realized there was a need for these topics to not only be discussed, but written about. As he interviewed other people involved, he found that the subject of grief went far deeper than he had ever realized. It was with this in mind that he started his trek into writing and speaking on these delicate issues. He currently speaks in both short engagements, as well as full length Thanatology seminars. His primary goal is to help others come to grip with their own grief, for whether a person's grief comes from death, divorce, dismemberment, paralysis, or any other means, the grief process is the same.

"Christ never promised us a life without conflict.
He did promise we could have peace in conflict."

–Ed Hamil

"To every thing there is a season,
and a time to every purpose
under heaven."

Ecclesiastes 3:1

Sonja Deanne Nevil Hardegree
1954 – 1994

DEDICATION

This book is lovingly dedicated in memory of my wife, Sonja D. Hardegree, who passed from this life on February 11, 1994 after a rather lengthy battle with cancer, at the age of 39 years, 4 months and 30 days. She was a kind, loving woman, the type woman many men dream of meeting and marrying, but especially, the kind of woman one could easily and joyfully grow old with. It is my deepest regret that I will not have that pleasure.

ACKNOWLEDGMENT

It is with my deepest heartfelt gratitude that I would like to thank the people at Hospice of Abilene for the warm, loving care they gave my wife during her fight with Cancer. I had heard of their services, yet it wasn't until we needed them that I truly understood what they do for the dying patients. It's not just your typical home health care. It's more, much more. There is an air of the deepest concern for what you and your entire family are going through. Perhaps it's because they've been there themselves, or maybe they've just become accustomed to it from working with the dying patients and their families, but whatever the case, you know from the first time they walk into your house, that the caring nature of these people is genuine.

THANK YOU:

Karen
Bettie
&
Lynda

WARNING – DISCLAIMER

It is the intent of the author in creating this book, to provide you with helpful ways through which you might better deal with a similar situation. While the events contained in this book are true as they happened to the author and his family, this book was not designed for use as a manual or guide in your analogous case. While you may want to mimic certain ways through which they coped, to see if they help you, it by no means should be used as, nor take the place of professional help. There are many support groups and Psychologists which are highly educated in this and other related fields, and should be consulted in these matters.

Neither the author, nor S.H.M. Publishing shall have liability nor responsibility to any person, who alleges either direct or indirect adverse emotional, psychological, and/or physical loss or damage due to the information contained in this book.

WARNING – DISCLAIMER

CONTENTS

FOREWORD

"All sorrows can be born," observed the writer Isak Dinesen, "if you put them into a story or tell a story about them."

In his book about the death of his wife Sonja, Greg Hardegree has done just that. Not a fictional story with just a nod to fact, but the true story of a beloved life and devastating loss.

Writing such an account has many benefits. Greg admits it's the way he's chosen to try to make sense of what seems to be a senseless loss. It's a story he shares with the earnest hope of helping others in similar circumstances move beyond pain, hopelessness, and tragedy. This is a document that will be of great importance to his children, grandchildren and other family members. And finally, it has given me a chance I might never have had otherwise to get to know Sonja Hardegree.

In my role as a hospice bereavement coordinator focusing on grief issues, sometimes I have the opportunity to really get to know the person who is dying. In other instances, death cuts short our relationship and it's the family to whom I grow close. Such has been the case with the Hardegrees.

Greg's memoir is a poignant testament to his wife and the family life they created together in the love of God. Their love, their faith and the stability of their family shines through these reflections as the sustaining force throughout the entire ordeal of Sonja's illness and death. He captures her strength and courage, her grace as she leaves their sons cherished letters to be read when they reach particular milestones in their lives. When Greg accepted the challenge of caring for Sonja, he did not merely perform a duty. He committed himself to easing her pain and suffering, to maintaining her dignity, and to loving her enough to let her go. His book resonates with unmasked emotions – anger, frustration, fear, sadness, peace – but ultimately, it is a remembrance of love and hope. It is with great pleasure and privilege, I recommend to you *When Death is Imminent.*

– Bettie Bowen, Hospice of Abilene

PREFACE

This book was written with the sincere hope that it will help to lighten the burdensome load of either a terminally ill patient or perhaps one of their family members. Neither place is one which I cherish the thought of living through again. If you fall into one of these two categories, let me assure you that my every thought and prayer is with you.

This book is one that mixes pain, sorrow, love, and extreme faith in the Lord Jesus Christ, with joy, happiness, and a lesson in how to grow with each. It is in our individual crises that we indeed do the most growing. You can experience profound growth in your love towards someone whom you thought you already deeply loved, and growth in your faith in God, no matter how close you already think you are in your relationship with him. Your entire outlook in everyday life can, if you will allow it, change for the better. Consider if you will, an athlete who has taken on the difficult task of training his body for a particular sporting event. How did he gain the strength to take on the task and win? Any muscle in the body will grow in strength as it is worked. The way a muscle is worked is by putting it under stress. When a muscle is stressed, it builds up a tolerance to the added pressure which in turn makes it stronger. The emotional and spiritual portions of our bodies are no different. When we are placed under emotional or spiritual stress, our beings will, out of necessity, become stronger. It's just as Newton's Law of Physics states: "For every action, there is an equal, but opposite reaction." On the other hand, just as the athlete can over stress his muscles, we too may over stress ourselves emotionally or spiritually. The trick is to channel your stress in ways which will best cause you to grow. The alleys through which this stress is channeled will vary from one person to the next, depending upon each individual's strengths and weaknesses. It is the intent of this author to possibly help you find your individual alleys and the best means by which you may use your stress for growth.

The Author

ONE

THAT YOU MAY KNOW
HER

I suppose each love song and every romance novel was written by a person who had a cherished lady or gentleman in mind. Perhaps they were real, or maybe just a figment of the author's imagination, but whichever the case, each time we hear that favorite love song, or read that intimate novel, it tends to bring to our minds someone who is, or was, the center of our lives. As we read or listen to these works of art, our emotions are stirred in ways through which we may sweetly reminisce, forgetting our everyday cares and worries, even if only for a while. There are certain songs which are meaningful to me, perhaps because they so fluently describe my now departed wife. To me, she was the woman portrayed in each meaningful love song , and every romance novel.

Sonja was a kind, beautiful woman, with a beauty that was not limited to her outward appearance, but that transcended far beneath the surface. She was the type person who had no enemies and treated everyone the same. Her eyes didn't measure a person by their financial status, education, nor by the way they dressed. Everyone had a uniqueness to her, a God given beauty which no one else on the face of this earth shared, and many times, only Sonja could see it. To her, every person, no matter how bad they appeared, had some good in them. She was a teacher in righteousness, though she didn't always know it. You see, Sonja didn't have a classroom except for the classroom of her example. Anyone who spent time with her, or even watched her could not help but become a better person. She just somehow had that effect on people. She loved people, but no one more than her family. To her two sons she was a mother, a playmate, and a friend. She was firm when she needed to be, but otherwise as gentle as a lamb. When the boys were younger, she would tell them bedtime stories which sounded as though she had read them from a book, but in actuality she made them up as she went. The boys would be spellbound, hanging on her every word and asking for more. Sometimes she would tell them several stories before they would go to sleep, and they always ended with a moral that taught them something. I believe her stories aided the kids in becoming more creative. They will surely never forget the stories she told. She was the mom portrayed in television commercials. The mom that every child dreams of having. The mom that puts even June Cleaver, or Carol Brady to shame.

Sonja and I met in the Intensive Care Unit of a hospital where we both worked. Sonja was a nurse, and I, a respiratory therapist. She was twenty-six and had never been married. She was waiting for that special someone and I was him. You will never know how thankful I am of that, for the best years of my life started when I met her. Until that time, everyone I dated was not quite what I wanted, and I thought perhaps I was setting my expectations too high, but Sonja was made just to order. We had the perfect relationship in every way. It was as though God had made her for me, and me for her. Everything was perfect. She was the one person who I was so comfortable with that every conversation just flowed. You remember how when you're with the wrong person you have to hunt for something to say. With Sonja it was just not that way. We had everything in common. We were soul mates, lovers, and best friends. She knew my innermost thoughts and I, hers. We worked together and played together. We laughed together and cried. Above any, our marriage was perfect. Perhaps you would better understand what she and I had if you read a poem I penned the week after we buried her:

MEMORIES

We had the best of everything,
in our relationship,
and all.
Our sons, our home,
and everything,
and our marriage could never fall.
Our love was the way
God meant it to be,
our vows were never forsaken;
then that dark and dreary
day came,
and by illness
my love, you were taken.

The days since your death
are pointless, it seems;
each new hour
brings no joy.
It seems the life
was taken from me,
and I'm a manikin,

or a toy.

I miss you so much
as you might know,
but the memories,
they abound.
I remember your
smiling face so dear,
in each sight,
and in every sound.

As I went through your things,
the memories,
they began to grow.
I could smell you
in your belongings, your clothes,
and the tears began to flow.

I miss you so much,
my wife, my love;
you were everything to me.
I shudder to think
of life alone;
how without you it will be;
but I pray to my God
that some day soon,
the sun will shine again,
and without you,
although the memories will stay,
my new life will soon begin.

--- --- --- --- --- --- ---

February 1994
Greg D. Hardegree

Sonja was perfect for me and I for her. We shared, we loved, we laughed and cried, and we're together still, even if only in memory.

Sonja exhibited the love of her Lord in her nature. This fact was displayed even to the end of her life. In her final few weeks, Sonja would hallucinate from the high quantities of Morphine she was receiving, yet even in her hallucinations she thought of others. She imagined people were in the room that in actuality were not, and would many times remark that they looked down on their luck. She would then ask one of us to go to the pantry and bring them food. In one such dream, Sonja asked me, "Honey, do you think that little girl is crying because her mother can't afford to feed her?" She then asked me if we had any money we could give them. Sonja's nature was surely one which all of us should exhibit in our everyday lives. She was a kind, gentle, loving woman who I will always deeply miss. She was the woman I always dreamed of growing old with, but regretfully, I will not have that pleasure.

TWO

THE BOMB SHELL

I guess there comes a time in everyone's life in which we each, from necessity, are forced to completely re-think the incredible infa-structure we so thoughtlessly call our lives. The true complexity of our lives; our emotions, our beliefs, our mental ability to merely cope, may in one swift moment be challenged, or even changed for the rest of life as we know it, yet even in the darkest hour of our deepest trial, we can find some form of solace. The trick, I suppose, is to somehow manage to keep your head above the water in a bottomless sea of anger, fright, sorrow, and endless emotions, by learning, as one does in a sea of water, to swim. As a child usually learns to swim with the use of some flotation device, we too must start by finding and donning some sort of emotional life preserver. In the beginning, you feel so lost in your feelings, and your future will seem so bleak that you will not realize you are sinking into this sea of emotional abyss.

I remember the despair, the feelings of being so out of control in an otherwise unchaotic life. A life in which I always had a solution to each and every problem dealt me in this game of existence, yet this time the cards were down and I had no ace in the hole. For the first few weeks after we found out my wife had cancer, this uneventful, usually predictable, and always enjoyable life was transformed into nothing short of pure chaos. We had the perfect marriage, two beautiful sons, good paying jobs, we spent time together as a family, and were involved in the church. We were as near the perfect family as any, yet one word echoed:

CANCER, CANCER, CANCER, and as this word echoed, it tore apart our perfect lives forever, and ushered in this vast sea of emotional chaos. For the first time in my life, I had no answers, I was as out of control as anyone could be. The thoughts were endless. What's the best form of treatment and where was the best place to get it? How would we afford it? How would we tell the boys and when? Why was this devilish, horrific disease plaguing us? Why not plague someone with a less than perfect marriage? The questions went on and on. A never ending tidal wave of unthinkable questions, with answers which were as far from our minds as was our next vacation. We would try to talk about these things yet the enormity of pain would somehow cloud our thought process, so the questions went unanswered and in turn ate a larger hole in our intestines. Don't get me wrong, I have a positive outlook on most anything, but these thoughts were spurred because we were told from the start that with her type cancer, there was no hope. The only thing we knew to be true was that there is a God in heaven and that through him all things are possible. There were only two things of a positive note which kept racing through my mind – "...All things work together for good to them that love God..." Romans 8:28 and the fact that everyone kept reminding me that God would not place more on me than I could bear. After several weeks of careful evaluation, and with a lump in my throat the size of Texas, I took my first real step towards my emotional life preserver with this prayer: "Lord God, if it is your will, heal my wife as only you can, and if it is not your will, help the boys and me to be able to bear the burden of this great loss." You see, I believe that God answers all prayers, even though the answers we receive may not be the ones we want. I have seen many people set themselves up for bigger heartaches and a loss of their faith by asking God to heal their loved ones, yet in their prayers they have incorporated invisible reins through which they try to narrow down God's impending answers to the ones they want. When they do not receive the answers they want, they blame God by saying, "Why is God doing this to me?" in turn, their faith begins a downward slide. Realizing this, and adjusting my prayers to remove these reins, I was placing the entire outcome of this ordeal in the Lord's hands, thus removing in a huge way, any guilt which might come in the end. This was a big step for me because I realized this battle could not even be fought without the help and assistance of one much more powerful than I, my maker and creator. As I pondered these things, I came to realize that I could only look for God's answers to my prayers with open expectations, knowing that his answers could be in any form. I remembered a story my Dad had told my wife several years before: "There was a man of great faith who was caught in a flash flood. As the water began to rise, it reached his door step. About this time, a man in a Jeep came by and told him, 'Get in, and I will take you to higher ground' yet the man refused saying, 'The Lord will save me.' The water continued to rise, and soon forced the man onto the roof of his house. At this time, a man in a boat paddled up and said, 'Get in and I will take you to safety' but again the man refused saying, 'The Lord will save me.' When the water was so high that he was forced into the treetops, a man in a helicopter came by to save him, yet again he refused for the same

9

reason. After the man drown he asked God, 'Lord, why did you not save me, I had complete faith in you?' The Lord replied, 'My son, I sent a man in a Jeep, but you refused. I then sent a man in a boat, and again you refused. As a last attempt I sent the helicopter, but you would not accept my answers'." As I remembered this story, I also remembered the many times in which I've seen people react this same way when God would answer their prayers in ways which they did not expect. I knew I could not allow myself, nor my family to fall into this faith destroying trap. The trick would be to constantly remind both them, and myself of this story, and to pray for the strength to both recognize his answers and to use them in the best way possible for our situation.

I realized that guilt had enormous potential. Potential to wreck my faith, my family, and to even destroy what little beauty might be left in the short time we had remaining as a complete family. I was determined to alleviate as many alleys of guilt as possible. There were areas which were obvious, and I was sure there were those which were not. Perhaps the initial awareness for possible guilt was that which was contained in Sonja's treatment vs. her outcome. I mean, how would I feel if I made the decisions for how her treatment would commence and with regard to which route it would take, and my decisions in actuality hurt her, or ended in regret? This indeed would have been a bitter pill for me to swallow and a decision which would have had long term repercussions that could have hindered me and my sons healing process. Definitely, all decisions with regard to her treatment had to be hers. This ridded me of any guilt of her deteriorating health, her suffering, or her death. I knew I could live knowing that we did it her way, once she was gone. I also had to leave to her the decision of when to call it quits, after all, I was willing to do anything she wanted towards her treatment, and we both realized that sooner or later, there would come the point at which the treatments were doing nothing more than prolonging misery. This decision, if made by me, could have had long lasting repercussions of guilt. The decisions were hers.

As medical people, Sonja and I had many times seen situations where due to the selfishness of a dying person's family, or even one family member, the dying patient was denied his or her last wish: to be allowed to die with some dignity, and without prolongation of their suffering by the use of mechanical life support. You see, although it is a law in most states that every person admitted to a medical facility must be informed of "Their Right to Die" or, "An Advance Directive," many people are unaware that there are loop holes built into this law, as there is in any law. Did you know that once you are in a comatose state, any one of your family members may over-ride your final wishes, even though you have them in writing? Too many times I've seen people's suffering last much longer than it should have because Mom or Dad, Brother or Sister wanted to hang on to their loved one a little longer. Once this attitude has been displayed, most doctors take this as a cue to initiate full heroics, thus depriving the patient of their dying wishes and prolonging their misery. It also places on the survivors a thick layer of guilt, which makes the healing process harder to cope with. Sonja and I were determined that we would not fall into this trap. She wanted to die at home and we were determined to allow her to do so.

The pressures of working through these things were enormous, but the one which haunted us most was when and how to tell the boys. The manner in which we break such news to a child could make the difference in how they cope, and timing is everything. Certainly they would grow acutely aware that their mom was becoming worse, after all, they were 11 and 8 years old, old enough to realize the difference between getting well and growing worse. But how do you tell a child his mom is dying, that he will have to live the rest of his life with only memories, and memories which would surely fade to a certain degree? The answer came on Christmas Eve. Sonja and I had spent the month at a pain clinic some three hours from home. With the boys only seeing us once during this period, and since this Christmas Eve was the day we returned home, we decided to open our gifts that night as a treat to the kids. The boys could always find something to fight about, and even in the excitement of the evening, a fight commenced. Without thinking about what she was saying, Sonja said, "Please don't fight. This may be our last Christmas together." The cat was out of the bag! Had this moment ruined our festive evening? It became so quiet you could hear a pin drop. Then the silence was broken when my older son said, "What do you mean by that, Mom?" The ball was rolling. In a flood of emotions, the subject was discussed, and in fact, that Christmas took on more meaning than any ever had. We all knew it would be our last Christmas together, and in the solemn, painful cheer of the evening, we grew. We were together, even if only for a few more fleeting moments in this life, at least we had each other then.

Sonja had cancer, and would die. This entire horrific bomb shell of immense proportion had been dropped on us, without any forewarning, without even a hint of its impending arrival. Although we had not been prepared for the shockwave this bomb emitted, we had somehow survived.

THREE

STOP AND SMELL
THE ROSES

In this hustle and bustle, live for the moment, and go for the gusto world we live in, we can easily become wrapped up in our modern day lives, filled with all the glamour of high paying jobs, fancy homes, and shiny cars. We have health clubs, golf courses, and dream vacations. We eat fine exotic foods, swim in our pools, or just sit in our air conditioned dwellings with forty or more channels from which to chose our entertainment, and yet we seek more. The more money we make, the more we want. The bigger our homes and cars, the larger still we dream of. The poor dream of becoming rich while the rich seek more riches. We have become so involved in our own personal gain that we have, in many instances, pushed aside the things which should truly be the center of our attention; our mates, our children, but above all our relationship with God. While we remain in search of a finer life, our marriages dissolve, our children grow up in emotionally unhealthy homes or perhaps end up on the streets or in prison from a lack of parental guidance, and yet we are blinded to the true cause of our failures. Our nature, is to blame anything or anyone else, but the blame is ours and so is the guilt. It's not society's fault, it's greed. Pure, unadulterated greed. While times are good, we by nature increase our debt, and we fail to realize a larger debt named responsibility. Responsibility to our mates and our children. The responsibility to provide them

15

with love, a nurturing love which creates bonding and closeness. A closeness which can transcend most anything, especially the trials of life. Perspective, that's the root of the problem. Somewhere along the line we have lost our focus. We have somehow made the not so important things important and have allowed the most important of all things to sink low on the list. Sadly, it sometimes takes a tragedy to bring into clearness our unfocused lives.

Somewhere amid the pain and agony of Sonja's illness it became clear that her cancer was a wilderness. Sure, that was the ticket! This was to be our wilderness. Just as God put good men through various wildernesses to bring them closer to him in the Bible times, this could just have been a trial which would aid us in our spiritual growth. I was partially right in this thought, but there was more to it than that. We not only grew spiritually, but our love for each other grew as well. Before the cancer, I thought my love for Sonja was as strong as it could possibly be. Certainly our marriage was the best of any I knew, but much to my surprise, our love grew just the same. The love for our children abounded as well. We cried together, and we grew. We shared our innermost thoughts, and we grew. We learned things about each other which we never knew. Our love grew in astronomical leaps, and we all changed. Our thoughts, our views, our ideas on most everything changed. We were the same people, yet somehow we were different, and this difference made us somewhat better. Not better than others, just better than we were before, closer to each other and closer to God. A closeness that would surely help us overcome whatever the future held. Whether good or bad, perhaps now we could overcome our largest obstacles together.

These new differences were everywhere, yet none were as obvious as the heightened awareness of our surroundings. In a way, we saw things through the eyes of babes. It was as though everything was a new experience. The pain and sadness were still there, but we looked at things so differently than before. Imagine if you will, what it would be like to be blind from birth, never being able to see the sunshine, clouds, flowers, or water, not knowing what green nor blue nor yellow were, and the beauty of the rainbow was only something you could imagine. But how could you imagine it, after all you don't even know what colors are, they too are only ideas toyed with in your head. You would never have seen your parents, nor could you see your mate, or your children. Photos and family videos would mean nothing. You would just live in your envious, troublesome world of darkness, seeing but little in comparison to others. Your world of darkness would go far beyond the darkness derived from the mere lack of light. Your's would be that frightful, lonesome darkness that comes from not knowing, that comes from within. While pondering these thoughts, consider the newness of your surroundings if after this lifetime of blindness, you could see. – That must be the sun! It's much bigger than I thought, and it's so bright! Could that be the color yellow? So that's trees! They're beautiful! They're nothing like I imagined, they're so tall! Wait, here comes someone. Could, could this be my, are you my, you're my son? After all the years of wanting to see your face I finally can, and you're much more handsome than I would have ever

17

imagined. – Do you understand the image I want you to see? It would surely seem somewhat miraculous to have your eyes opened to such beauty after knowing nothing but darkness your entire life. This, in a since was what Sonja and I were experiencing. Of course not to this degree, but there is something about a tragedy which is an eye opener. As the tears began to subside, our eyes beheld the beauty which was always there, yet we never saw. Somehow, we had before missed the true beauty of a sunrise, a gentle breeze, or the flowers of springtime. The reds were redder, the blues were bluer, and white was never so white. The freshness of rain seemed somewhat fresher and the songs of the birds seemed so much sweeter. Perhaps before we were only seeing with our eyes, and now, somehow, this illness made us see with our hearts. Whatever the cause, we now saw clearer and crisper, with a beauty that left us awe-struck. It all brought to mind the true power of our God, after all, if he held the power to create this big world and all it's beauty, he surely had the power to heal Sonja, if only it were his will. In some simple way, our new visions of beauty brought on a new kind of faith. Not a blind faith that made us believe she would wake up in the morning and be free of this dreaded disease. No, it was somehow a more tangible faith than we had ever experienced. Not that we could see God, but that we could see more clearly his magnificent power in everything which surrounded us. We realized this world in it's infinite beauty did not just happen. It was by no means an accident, and if God loved us enough to create all this for us, he would surely see us through this difficult ordeal. God did not cause this disease to happen, after all, cancer runs high in Sonja's family. She had lost both Grandmothers to cancer, and one, she had even nursed unto death. Sonja's cancer was the product of genetics, and God allowed it to happen. Not out of cruelty, out of love. You see, I believe that God in his infinite wisdom saw that our family would grow through this wilderness, and surely he had a purpose in her death. We cannot always see his purpose, but in everything he does, or allows, there is one, and at the end of the long dark tunnel of our wildernesses we may emerge better and stronger than before. Whatever God's purpose, we will someday know, and until then we must exercise patience and look for the good in everything that is bad, for in this we grow.

Life is truly just a fleeting moment in time. We're born, we live, we die, and once we die we are just a memory, a memory that time will surely fade. In everything we do, we make memories. We are remembered in good or in bad, in our selfishness or sharing. We are remembered with pleasure or dislike, in tears or spite. Whatever the case, the memories we leave are all that is left when we're gone. As we live in this hurried world of endless material pleasures, let's not forget to focus on what we may take with us, or what we'll leave when we die. The next time you're pressed for time, in a hurry to meet that next client, or to close that deal, remember first to "stop and smell the roses", for once the rose has withered, the sweet aroma will still be a memory for awhile.

FOUR

GESTURES OF
LOVE

There is a saying which states, "when the going gets tough, the tough get going," but how many times does this mean that when the going gets tough, the tough take off the other direction? You can only tell who is loyal to you and who will stand with you in your time of need, when a crisis arises. I'm not just talking about friends, but family, relatives, children, and even your mate. Sadly, there are times when the people we thought we were closest to, disappear when we need them the most. Husbands have left wives, parents have left children, and friends have found new friends for no other reason than to keep your new burden from affecting their lives. Perhaps I shouldn't use the word "burden," for when you truly love someone, no matter the situation, they are never a true burden, but rather, a minor inconvenience through which you both mature in your love. You see, there is a certain joy which lasts a lifetime that comes from devoting yourself completely to the care of your dying loved one. Remember the feeling you get when you give someone something that makes them happy? This is also true, but even to a greater degree when the gift you gave was yourself. The care of loved ones in this situation is at the very least, exhausting, when it is done right, yet the rewards are endless once you are through.

Sonja was the type person who put people above all

else. There was a time when she was still nursing which I remember so vividly, perhaps because it was a window through which you could see into the deepest portions of her ever loving and caring soul. This night Sonja was assigned a dying patient in the Intensive Care Unit of our hospital, and as you might imagine, Sonja believed that a person should not be alone at their dying moment. It was not a belief she was taught, nor one she learned from example, but she believed it just because she was sweet, loving, caring Sonja. That night, after Sonja was off work, she stayed by the comatose woman whom she didn't even know, except for her name. She sat there for several hours simply holding this woman's hand. Why? So the woman wouldn't leave this world alone. Medical people, in time, tend to become insensitive or hardened from working so closely with death and dying, but not her. I think perhaps we could all take a lesson from the radiant loving nature which she possessed. This nature was perhaps the first thing that attracted me to her, for she loved me unconditionally, with a depth as deep as a black hole. If Sonja would be there for a total stranger in her dying hour, then no matter what it took, I was determined that I would be there in Sonja's dying hour. As I said before, there is no greater gesture of love than to commit yourself to the total care of especially your mate, after all, isn't this even included in your oath of matrimony? Too many times this promise is conveniently forgotten when a spouse most needs his or her mate. Consider the guilt felt in the end by those who abandoned their loved ones in the most physically and emotionally painful time of their life. They gave them no moral support, nor any help with even the most basic physical needs as the disease process stripped them of their ability to even keep themselves bathed or go to the bathroom in private. Put yourself in this situation. How would you feel? I suggest that most anyone would prefer their mate to help them with these potentially embarrassing areas than for a total stranger in the health field to enter into their home and do these things for them. Yet, if their mate has abandoned them the strangers will help, thus removing any dignity they may have left. In the end, the mate who abandoned his or her loved one can only reflect back with wishes of having done more. This guilt may very well prolong the healing process.

When caring for your mate, don't forget to include your children, no matter how young they may be, for this too will aid them in their healing process. Sure they cannot do a lot of the things that will need to be done, but surprisingly, they can be more help than you may now realize. There were times in my wife's illness in which I might go several days without any sleep, or at the most, catch short naps of ten to fifteen minutes. My oldest son, who was 11 at the time, started rotating nights with me which allowed me to recharge myself. Jerrod would sleep on a mattress on the floor next to Sonja. When she would need something, she would either reach out and touch him or perhaps call out to him and he would be there for her. This switching of nights was Jerrod's idea and I believe it did him as much good as it did Sonja and me, for today, almost ten months after her death, Jerrod still remembers his helping role with fondness. Being there for his mother, I believe, has helped him deal with his mother's death. Christopher, our eight year old, was continually fluffing pillows, bringing medicine, and generally hovering over her to insure that her every need was well taken care of.   Although this 24 hour a day care was work, it was also rewarding, for in the end, the boys and I could say, "If we had it to do over again, we would do it the same way". We had no guilt.

There is a flip side to every coin, while you do what you can, when you need to, there are times in which it may become too much to handle. If this happens, don't let it discourage you. Only God Almighty himself can do all, and when the time comes that you need help in your task, take heart, there are those who will help. I'm not just talking about Hospice or home health agencies, but family members or friends. Sonja's mother was a big help throughout those long months. She would help with getting the kids off to school, with Sonja's baths, bed changes, and would stay with her while I worked the few days I could. There were more people, some I didn't even know, that helped with finances, meals, and the kid's Christmas. The people I worked with had bake sales, car washes, and the like to raise money to help. The church bailed us out on more than one occasion and helped us with the enormous medical bills. I remember thinking how a crisis shows you just how many good, caring people this old world still has in it despite the high crime rate and low moral values. I can never thank those people enough for all they did.

As you suffer through your hard times, always remember to give your best, no matter how hard it may seem, for the gestures of love you display during these times are perhaps the most cherished and definitely the most rewarding. Giving will only help you to heal in the end if you give from the heart.

FIVE

TAKE MY ADVICE

Free advice is everywhere in a time of crisis, but indeed you get what you pay for. There are always those who, although they mean well, can in their over zealous endeavor to come to your aid, make matters worse. Sometimes this advice is meant to somehow help you through your tough spot, but other times it is nothing more than a way for another hurting person to deal with their own similar crisis by talking it out with you. Others still, bask in their own past pain. After years in the medical field there is one thing I have noticed, there are those who enjoy talking about themselves, their heartaches, or their illnesses so much that they forget you may have all the problems you can handle at the moment without listening to their's. There was one woman who sent us several cards during this ordeal and they each started with, "Thinking of you" then was proceeded with at least one page of this woman's ailments, from her newest hangnail, to the time she had her first surgery one hundred eons ago. You tell me. Was this woman's first statement genuine? Did she really care about my wife and the situation we were living in, or were we just another ear to bend? Another woman, one of the second above mentioned cases, was promptly at my wife's side, the day after Sonja found out she had cancer, and commenced telling Sonja how badly her husband suffered with his cancer before he died. Yeah, that's precisely what you want to hear after you've just found out you have the big C. As a general rule, I've noticed that people are usually only sensitive when it comes to their own problems. It's kind of like the difference between major and minor surgery; major surgery is when it's happening to you, and minor surgery is when it's on someone else.

Besides those who are always willing to bestow upon you their problems at the worst possible time, there are those who give advice and make suggestions, some of which sound like they came from the stone age. Please, take my advice and don't take any advice. You see, every case of cancer, like most illnesses, are totally different. While some may cause pain, others leave you relatively pain free. While some may end in death, others are totally and completely curable. The disease process is also vastly effected by each individual, their pain tolerance, their overall health at the beginning, and yes, even the persons own outlook about their situation makes a difference in the outcome. I have seen those who die for no other reason than they believed they would. I remember a man in our hospital who I am convinced passed from this life because he felt he didn't have a life to go home to. There was basically nothing medically wrong with him and certainly nothing that would have killed him, yet he died because he gave up on trying, because he wanted to die. The attitudes we have, markedly make a difference in our healing process. There are those which the doctors have given little or no chance of survival but have, to everyone's astonishment, pulled through and even become well. In every such case, it was due to the patient's positive attitude. The people you choose to listen to can mean the difference in your having a positive or negative attitude and can directly affect your outcome.

While listening to the massive amounts of advice you will surely receive in your ordeal, listen with courtesy, and if you absolutely have to, be curt. Some people will help with their advice, but others can only hurt you. It boils down to your own decisions in the end anyway. If someone suggests trying an African witch doctor because they feel they had success with him, they can't make the decision to go to Africa for you. No, this was not someone's advice to Sonja, but believe me, we heard some just as ridiculous, and we weighed what seemed to be sound advice and rejected the crazy suggestions. The only thing that matters is that you are comfortable with your decisions, for the outcome will effect you, not the advice givers. It is for this reason that you must be comfortable with what you decide.

Another area that chaps my hide is the audacity some people have to use your bad situation for their own financial gain. Specifically, there was a funeral home operator who would frequently send us cards. So what's the problem? These cards were not bought by him out of love and concern for us, they were funeral home cards, complete with his personal business card inserted. In other words, he was waiting like a buzzard for my wife to die so he could get our business. Needless to say, he didn't get it. While these ruthless people prey on those less fortunate individuals in a crisis, it is important to remember that you are in charge. While these people will make you mad, try not to let them ruin an already bad time. Simply remember that one day the tables will be turned, and they will learn first hand the rudeness they once displayed towards you and how it made you feel.

Allow me to say at the close of this chapter that although we were extremely religious people, there were at times those with different religious views who came forth to lend a religious hand. This is not bad in itself, but I should make you aware that some things people will want to do could possibly hinder your healing process in the end. What I am talking about is this: Do not allow anyone to do anything of a religious nature for you nor with you that will cause you to be uncomfortable. You see, when you allow something which you can't completely agree with, you are leaving yourself open for a kind of spiritual guilt. Some people feel in the end that perhaps things might have turned out differently had they stuck to their own religious ways of doing things. Let me say at this point that this was not the case with Sonja and me because such feelings are usually derived from the belief that God will punish you for things you do or don't do while you are still on this earth. You see, we believe that God doesn't punish you for your actions here on earth. If he did there would be no need for Hell. If you are one who believes God punishes you while on this earth, may I strongly encourage you to not partake in the things people will ask you to, unless you 100% agree with them. In the end I believe you will find it more comforting.

SIX

PREPARING FOR THE END

Although you may not believe it, as time goes on and the shock of finding the disease begins to subside, your cloudy vision will soon began to clear. Things tend to become easier to deal with and to talk about. The realness of the impending death sinks in and in your new clearer sight, you realize the time has come to prepare for the end. As you realize this time has come, it is easy to allow a flood of thoughts to rise like a weed and choke you. There were things which Sonja wanted to do, and things which she wanted to say before it was too late. She became so very frantic in her endeavor to do all these things that she at times seemed like a shark in a feeding frenzy. I suppose this would happen in any such case. I had to remind her that these things might be better accomplished if she would slow down and set up an orderly way of achieving these goals.

As you might imagine, Sonja's first concern was for her family. She seemed to somehow feel that we would soon forget her and she wanted to give us all something to remember her by. Although these things mean a great deal to us now, there is not, nor will there ever be a day to go by that we won't remember her in fondness. Just the same, she was determined to give each of us a token of remembrance. To Christopher, she gave a crystal Blue-bird of Happiness with her instructions to him to always remember her and know she remembers him and loves him each time he looks at it. Recently, when the kids

29

were to bring their most prized possession to school for show and tell, Christopher took his blue bird of happiness. There have been many times in which I've observed him gently polishing this crystal bird since his mother's death. To Jerrod, Sonja gave a Gerber tool which contained several tools and knives in one. She knew that he was too old to receive anything of a sentimental nature like Christopher's blue bird, so she chose a "manly" gift. With it was again her instructions to use it in her remembrance. She knew that I was struggling with whether to bury her with her wedding rings on or keep them. It was for this reason that she instructed her sister to buy a gold chain for her to give to me so I could wear our rings around my neck. Sonja gave this to me and said she wanted me to keep them close to my heart. Below is what she wrote on the card that accompanied the chain:

To My Everlasting Love,

Our rings are a symbol of
our love, which has no end.
Wear them close to your heart
that you may cherish all the
wonderful things we have
shared together and yet have
to share in the time ahead
which has no end.

With My Unending Love,
Sonja

I know it may seem silly, but sometimes the things we struggle with the most are the things which are the smallest in nature, such as whether or not to bury her with her rings. Sonja will never know how much she helped me in this simple, but difficult decision. Thus Sonja continued giving to family and friends little gifts of remembrance.

Sonja was determined to continue to be a mother to her two sons as much as possible even in her death. Several weeks before she died, Sonja started writing letters to her boys. These were not just ordinary letters, they were letters which were to be opened at specific times in their lives. You see, Sonja wanted the boys to feel as though she was going to continue to be in their lives even though she was gone. Her first letter was to be opened after her funeral. It was a letter of encouragement to them to overcome their sadness and to continue on in their life. Below is a copy of this first letter:

January 21, 1994

Dear Boys,

I just wanted you to know that I love
you both so much and let you know
that even though I am gone now, I
will always love you and care about you.
If there is any way possible for me to
look down from above and watch you
grow up, I will. Please don't blame
God for what happened to me
because it was not him that made
me sick. The sickness just happened
and God will use it for his purpose.

Please, just remember that I
am happier now than I could
ever have been on earth
because now I am not only
with God, but also with my
grandparents and Grandpa
Conaway, and if you will
always follow God's will, we
will be together again too.
Be happy for me and remember
that I love you both.

With all my love,
Mom

This was the first of several letters which she wrote for the kids. The others were written for each one to open on their 13th birthday, because this is an important time for a child. After all, that's the beginning of the teen years. Her next letters were for each to open on their 16th birthday, for that is the age of the driver's license. Next we have the letters to be opened on their graduation day, then one for their wedding day, and finally one for the day that their first child is born. I believe that there are many people who could take a lesson from Sonja. She refused to become swallowed up by self pity. Instead of using what time she had left to feel sorry for herself, she used the time to help those who would survive her. This was perhaps our greatest gift from her.

Around five weeks before her death, Sonja woke up one morning and said, "Sweetheart, today you need to go down to the funeral home and make all the arrangements for my funeral." Although this was a shocking way to say good morning, I knew she was right. I'd just been refusing to think about it. In her calm foresight, Sonja helped me over yet another hump. She knew it would be easier for me to take care of this task while she was still alive, than to wait until all time had slipped by. There was another advantage to this. It insured that we would carry out this final memorial precisely as Sonja wished. She picked out every detail as though she had given a lot of thought to it all. She knew the flowers she wanted, the songs to be sung, the dress she wanted to be buried in, and who she wanted to be pallbearers. The flowers she picked for the spray were Sonia Roses with Babies Breath. I knew in an instant why. These were the flowers in her wedding bouquet more than a decade ago. After her death these were also the flowers we placed in the vase on her head stone. The only decision I had to make was the casket she was to be buried in. She said she didn't want a lot of money to be spent on one, but this was my one contribution to the whole service, so I chose a nice one. After all, when you think about it, funerals are actually for the survivors and not the dead.

About the time things took a turn for the worse, we discussed the legalities involved in a persons right to die, and their right to die with dignity in the privacy of their own home. With the experiences we had in the medical field, we knew the only safe way to insure that she could die as she wanted, was to sign power of attorney over to me. What people don't understand is this, when you go to a hospital you lose the full right to make decisions about your death. As I said in an earlier chapter, even a "Living Will" can be overridden by either a family

33

member or even your doctor, and believe me when I say, there are many doctors who believe their oath of medicine doesn't include allowing a patient to die. Many believe that it is their duty to take all measures in saving your life even if it's not your wishes. These doctors will lead you to believe they will follow your wishes when the time comes, but in actuality they never intend to do any such thing. Knowing this, Sonja signed over all rights to me, thus insuring that my decisions would carry great weight. We also took this time to make sure our wills were in order. Are you aware that in the event both you and your spouse die leaving minor children, that unless you both have "Wills", the state will decide what will happen to your children? This means that your kinfolk will not necessarily get custody of your children. The state could very well place them in foster homes, possibly splitting them up. Consider how much more traumatic it would be for a child who has just lost both parents to find out they weren't even going to get to live with grandma and grandpa, but instead would have to go live with strangers. May I strongly urge you to make out a will if you haven't already done so. Be sure that you both state who is to take custody of your children in the event you do both die. Such a small task can give you much peace of mind.

Take every opportunity to prepare for the end, for every preparation made in advance will make the end easier to bear. You will also find comfort in knowing you did everything in accordance to the dying person's will, and they will find comfort in knowing they helped lighten your forthcoming load.

SEVEN

LIVING AFTER DEATH

After all the preparations had been made, the weeks seemed to go by a little faster. Perhaps because the burden of planning for the end was no longer hanging over our heads, or maybe we were just a little more adjusted to what we knew lay ahead. Whatever the case, it seems that Sonja's health started declining rapidly after that. It took more drugs to keep her comfortable, her urine output began to taper, and she was slipping in and out of consciousness more frequently. Soon after that, the unconscious periods were lasting longer than the conscious. I have often thought this was, to a very large degree, a blessing for Sonja. The week starting February the 6th, Sonja went into a coma and remained there until the night before she died. On that Thursday evening, Sonja awoke for the last time. She couldn't see anything, but she knew I was there when she heard my voice. I was unaware she was awake until I heard her say, "Hi Sweetheart". I said "Hi" and asked her if she wanted to see the boys. At her affirmative answer, I summoned the boys to the bedroom. Perhaps the sweetest and most meaningful words my boys will ever hear were then spoken in Sonja's final words that night. With the boys hands in hers, Sonja repeated three times these final words: "I love you so much and I'm so proud of you". With this said, she slipped into her final comatose state. The following night at ten minutes after eight, our beloved wife and mother died. The sweetest of all God's creatures was gone, and already we missed her deeply.

There were family and friends for the next several days, with a constant stream of people into my now broken home. In actuality, these people surrounding us were a blessing, for once the funeral was over and the people began to leave, reality hit. My wife, the person I loved the most was gone. The person I wanted to grow old with had left this world for a better place, and now I would have to grow old without her. Why, when I had the most perfect marriage of any, did this thing have to happen, stripping me of my most prized possession? Although I am told these feelings are normal, there is a certain degree of guilt that can accompany them. When you think about it, perhaps these thoughts are on the selfish side, but just the same they were there.

The adjustment after the death of someone so near and dear to you can take the form of many things. I suppose it is different for every individual, for after all, the circumstances of every relationship vary so greatly. Everyone told me the first year was going to be the toughest, and once we had made it through that, it would become easier. I cannot tell you whether it does or not for I am not through that first year as yet. It has only been ten months since Sonja died. I can however, tell you that while it hasn't been easy by any means, it has been a growing experience for both the boys and me. While we miss her deeply, I do feel the days are becoming little by little easier to face. While the adjustment process has been slow, we are becoming accustomed to being the three musketeers, sticking together because we all realize that each other is all we have.

As I said before, your healing process can take many forms. For some, it is best to seek counseling in order to cope. For others still, it may be group therapy with those who have been through similar circumstances. I know there are many such groups available through either Hospice or some churches. Whichever means are best for you, can only be decided by you. As for myself, I chose to deal with my new life by writing. If I feel I may help someone with something I say, it can only help me. Besides, thinking back over our recent past helps me to put it all into perspective. As I ponder these things, words tend to come to me and I feel an urge to write them down. This has been my outlet.

It seems that with each changing season, I have gone through my toughest times. For some reason these changes have had a larger emotional impact on me than most holidays have. Perhaps that's because each one that comes brings closer the end of that first year without Sonja. Whatever it is, I have dealt with them by writing about them. Such is the poem below which I penned during one such changing season:

YEARNINGS

The days are sunny
and springtime has sprung,
but my life is
still full of grief.
I remember you often
in fondness and tears,
at our life so lovely
but brief.

Will the pain go away,
will the sadness end,
or will it continue to stay?
It makes me wonder
what life has in store,
as I struggle
from day unto day.

As I try to heal
the hurt that I feel,
since I buried you
Valentines Day,
the emptiness I feel,
and the void so real
just won't seem to go away.

I dream of you nightly,
with dreams upon dreams,
their so sweet, yet they
never stay;
for I open my eyes
at the end of the night,
just to face another
grim day.

I long for the day
when our eyes meet again,
and our arms
can warmly embrace.
But my work on this earth
has not yet been done,
so with tears
I shall finish this race.

But one grand day
we will meet again
and talk over times
past out parting;
then things will be
as they were before,
when our life together
was starting.

--- --- --- --- --- --- --- ---

April 1994
Greg D. Hardegree

The springtime was hard. For some reason, the waking of the trees and flowers were not as beautiful without Sonja to share it all with. I tried to fill our spring and summer with many fun things to help the kids keep their minds off their great loss. Although it seemed to help, there was still something missing. Something that constantly nagged us and kept us from enjoying things to their fullest. We did make it through the summer though, and perhaps it was even a little easier than we had first anticipated. Perhaps that's the way it is with all holidays as well. It could very well be that the worst part of any holiday during your first year is nothing more than the mere anticipation of having to face another one without your loved one. At any rate, once they are over, you usually look back on them with a sigh and say, that wasn't so bad. It always helps to remember that the rest of the family will be there and although you are all hurting, the holidays also bring times of remembrances and sweet stories about the deceased. There is something about listening to another family member talk lovingly about your now departed loved one that helps you through, and

39

even makes you enjoy that day you so dreaded to see coming. As these holidays approached, my thoughts again began to flow. As they poured forth I wrote this:

THOUGHTS OF LOVE

Nine months have now passed
since I lost you my love,
but I think of you daily
e'en still.

I remember the time
that our love was anew,
and my heart with your beauty
did fill.

How we looked at each other
with eyes for the other,
and our hearts were excited
and thrilled.

Our minds were full
with the wonders of love,
and nothing could make us
stand still.

As we walked together,
we laughed and we played,
and our love grew from day
unto day;

our enormity of love,
was a tide from above,

like waters rolling
into the bay.

But though you are gone
my memories are clear;
in my heart they will
always be cherished;

and though I will age
without you, my love,
I pray the memories
won't perish.

--- --- --- --- --- --- --- ---

November 1994
Greg D. Hardegree

It's funny how certain days will cause memories to flood one's mind. The memories of one day may be vastly different from the memories of the next. While we all three have memories which we are fond of, it seems that all too often we remember the things which we would rather not. According to Bettie Bowen, the Bereavement Coordinator and dear friend, whom I met through Hospice of Abilene, remembering all too clearly the look of pain on the face of your dying loved one, or their deteriorating health, or perhaps the helplessness the disease withered them to, is a common process which people go through as they heal. As time goes on, these bad memories will fade and be replaced with the sweet essence of the good memories we all hold so dear to our hearts. I can certainly see the truth in Bettie's statement. While the bad memories show up less than they did a few months ago, they do from time to time resurface. I

41

suppose that although we have these unpleasant memories, they do serve a purpose. I can see my wife in her final state and even though it hurts, it reminds me of the outstanding care my boys, my mother-in-law, and I gave her. This could easily reflect back to a previous chapter in this book, because you can only achieve this ability to see the good among the bad if you stand by your mate as you promised in your wedding vows. As I said in that chapter, the care you give or the lack thereof, will directly affect your individual healing process. If you feel good about what you did for your loved one while they were alive, by the same token you will feel better when you remember those times, and the emotional mending will soon begin.

The quicker you begin to heal, the quicker too, your children will heal. You see, your children's healing process, though similar to yours, can depend heavily on how they see you adjusting. If you sit around feeling sorry for yourself, and doing generally nothing besides sulking, your children will also become somewhat lethargic in life. When we pick ourselves up by the bootstraps, dust ourselves off, and try to put together the pieces of our shattered lives, our children will also follow suit. It can also work in reverse to a certain degree. Children somehow tend to adjust easier than do the adults. Many times I've noticed that a child will become ill in a shorter period of time than an adult, but the virus generally will also subside in a shorter period of time. It's the same with a child's emotions. Also, one thing I noticed is how much quicker my younger son has seemed to heal than my older one. For instance, while my older son has stated that he doesn't want to put up a Christmas tree, nor decorate this year, my younger son quickly became so wrapped up in the thrill of it all that it seems this holiday season will be no different in his eyes than any before. Perhaps this is why Christ used children as examples so frequently in his ministry. While an adult has trouble keeping focused on the important things in life, the children have complete faith that all will remain well, no matter the situation. I remember a time when Jerrod was two. I had him standing on the hood of the car. Without any forewarning, Jerrod leapt from the car towards me as though he thought he could fly. While I was unprepared for this child's adventure in faith, I did, lucky for him, catch him. I believe this to be the perfect example in faith for us all to consider. You see, Jerrod had full faith that I wouldn't let anything bad happen to him. He had the kind of faith in me that we all should have in Christ. A total, undoubting, never ending faith. I suspect when we finally develop this kind of faith that our troublesome times will become much easier to bear.

While we all must find the best way to cope with, and adjust to our individual losses, let's not forget that we are not alone in our grief and pain. If you need help, seek help. Surrounding yourself with those who also are hurting can sometimes make you realize that your pain is not so severe. Be strong for your kids and they will be strong for you. Try to find the good in what is happening, for the good is there, although it is sometimes hard to find. Embrace the good memories and the bad ones will soon began to fade. Above all else, keep a strong faith in the Lord, for this will help you more than anything.

EIGHT

YOU HAVE MY PERMISSION

Although the human machine is complex and complicated, it is sometimes the little things which influence us the most. What drives one person's emotions, may have no effect on another's. What may mildly spur an emotional response in one, may in fact violently erupt the emotions of another. Whether consciously or subconsciously, these emotional triggers are there, and they play a major role in our lives, and yes, even in our deaths. Emotions are triggered in happiness and in sadness, in times of fright, and in our braver moments, but sometimes our emotional beings are in need of help, a help which can be derived through either words or actions. These words or actions may not be earthshaking, but simple and kind, or perhaps just of an encouraging nature. The words I am thinking of at the moment are four little words which we have heard all our lives, yet when spoken at the right time, and in the proper context of the situation, may make our emotional pitfalls easier to live with. These four little words are, "you have my permission".

As children, we were all taught to ask permission when the situation dictates. Perhaps it all started as a means of teaching us there is a certain degree of respect which is due our elders, or maybe it was to teach us to respect other people's property. Which ever the case, these principles last us a lifetime. When we became teenagers, full of assertive, sometimes defiant means of testing our limits and trying our wings, we still held in the back of our minds a continuous knowledge that we needed our parents permission on certain issues. As young adults, our wings were fully spread, yet we were not always comfortable with certain decisions we were faced with, and so, there we were, in essence, asking for our parents permission, wanting their approval. We needed this security to fully feel confident in our decisions. I remember the first time I bought a house. I knew the place was affordable, I knew it was in good shape, and I knew the interest rates being down meant it was the right time to buy, but still, I couldn't quite bring myself to make the final decision without first checking with my dad. Although in my mind I was not asking for his permission I was indeed doing just that. After all, this practice had been instilled in me since my birth. Aren't we all this way to a degree? When you marry, this process of giving and receiving permission continues. When either spouse wants to make a rather large purchase, we first invent ways to sell the idea and need for this usually unneeded object to our mate..."Just think dear, we could have more family time if we bought this boat," or "your meals would never be late again if I could only have that new microwave oven." Let's face it, aren't we just asking for permission? Don't get me wrong, I'm not saying this is bad, I'm just trying to demonstrate how important this concept of permission is. It affects us throughout our lives even though we usually fail to realize it. The concepts of gaining or giving permission is as thick as trees in a forest throughout our lives. It is present not only in our personal lives, but in our schools, our jobs, and even in our government. We cannot escape this simple but powerful part of our social make up.

With terminal illnesses, this permission can play an important part in our coping power after the loss of a loved one, or can even help the dying during their actual death. This may seem somewhat foreign to you, but let me explain. Sonja was an extremely jealous woman. From even the time when we were dating, this was true. Although some might think this to be a bad characteristic, I loved it. I remember one time in particular. Sonja and I were to go to my home town for a visit with my parents. It was to be the first time for Sonja to meet them. The day came, and Sonja came down with a stomach virus. Needless to say, she was unable to go. She told me to go ahead without her and I did. It was one of the most miserable days of my life. After driving an hour to get there, I visited for maybe five minutes before leaving, and during that five minutes I made a call to Sonja to check on her. She was so much a part of my life, the visit was meaningless without her, so I returned to see her. When I arrived, I promptly picked up one of her hair brushes and quickly groomed my beard before I entered her sick room to see her. THAT WAS A BIG MISTAKE, for when I used her hair brush, one of her long reddish brown hairs decided to take up residence in my beard. Of course, the hair didn't hide itself well and Sonja found it, immediately assuming it was the hair of my ex-girlfriend back home. I don't have to tell you what happened next, suffice it to say, it took three days for her to come to her senses and forgive me. The only reason she forgave me then was because one of the nurses at work pulled a hair from Sonja's head and asked her, "Did that hair you found in Greg's beard look anything like this one?" I wish I'd thought of doing that! Knowing now how jealous Sonja was, you will now be able to understand this:

47

When you lose your mate, you many times have no intention of getting remarried, although this is not something which we completely control. You must understand, after living for so many years with a jealous woman, you tend to develop the mind set that in the event you lost her, you could never remarry, for she would never forgive you, and perhaps even in a sense haunt you for the rest of your life if you did. In such cases as ours, there is a form of solace in the giving of permission to the survivor to remarry. Much to my surprise, towards the end, Sonja did just that. It was about ten days before she died. We were talking about the end when she suddenly announced, although with a lump in her throat, "Greg, when I am gone, I want you to know that it's alright for you to remarry. I won't mind." There have been many times since her death that I have remembered this, and it does have a somewhat calming effect when I think about my future. I'm not hunting for another mate, but if the right one comes along, I can start a new relationship without the burden of great guilt. If another one ever does begin, this too will help the new relationship to be successful.

Earlier I said that permission can play a beneficial part on behalf of the dying person in their death. Allow me to now explain. Years in the medical field has taught me one thing, many people, although sometimes comatose, will many times hang on to life, in all it's misery, for someone they love. You see, although a person may be in a comatose state, they many times can still hear. Just because they are in a coma doesn't necessarily mean that they have no level of consciousness. Never under estimate the power of the sub-conscience. During the last week of her life, Sonja entered deaths door more than once, only to return and wait until another day. The first such time was an evening that the children were home. Sonja was obviously mere moments away from death, when the boys started to cry and say, "Please don't die mom." When I review my mind's video of that evening, it becomes clear that the only thing that made her return was her obvious pity on her two sons. Another such event happened later in the week when her brother was there. Again she snatched herself from the grips of death to allow her brother some solace. To show you how near death she was before returning, Karen, one of the nurses for Hospice who was there at the time this happened, stated: "In all my years of nursing, I have never before seen anyone come that close to dying and return." We talked about these two events and decided that Sonja was merely hanging on for the sake of her upset family. We decided the next time this happened, we would clear the room of all who were crying, and that I should give her my permission to die. That Friday evening, as Sonja again entered the door of death, I held her hand and said, "Sonja I love you, but it's all right for you to die. You have suffered long enough." Three minutes later, with her hand still in mine, she took her last breath. How important was my giving her permission to die? I think it meant the difference in whether or not she would have died that night.

As you travel down the bumpy troublesome road of terminal illness, keep a strong faith in the Lord. Remember to take your every concern to him in prayer, for in this we gain our strength. Use your family and friends to help you through the tough days, and remember, not all the days will be tough. Your love can grow, your awareness of the true beauty of life can increase, and you can be more prepared for whatever befalls you, no matter how bleak your future may seem. The beauty of life doesn't end in the death of a loved one, but the memories we carry on can be made more precious by the way we live those last priceless days. Remember the importance of giving and receiving permission, and your emotions will heal quicker than you think. Above all, remember that God blesses us in our trials, although it doesn't always seem that way.

NINE

COUNTING OUR BLESSINGS

With all the down days involved in being, or caring for the terminally ill, it is sometimes hard to see any good among the bad. We are supposed to focus on the good surrounding us, but sometimes it seems somewhat impossible to do. We sing songs in church about counting our blessings, but how many times are these just idle words coming from our mouths and not meaningful words from our hearts? Is it even possible to learn to focus on the good things in our lives, during the times there is so much bad around us? I believe the possibilities are there. We must only learn to restructure our thought processes.

I have a mentally handicapped Cousin who for years worked at a local cafeteria. His father, my Uncle, was an insurance salesman. Like most of us, My Uncle woke up one morning, dreading the day of work which faced him. As he went through his daily ritual of showering, shaving, and the like, he was also uttering soft complaints about the day which lay ahead. About this time, my Cousin spoke up and said, "But Daddy, we are sure lucky to have jobs." He was right, and my Uncle knew it. Needless to say, this honest statement from his son changed the outlook he had on his day. Perhaps the secret to restructuring our outlook, is to be found in the attitude my cousin took towards their jobs. After all, if they hadn't

51

had jobs, there lives would have been completely different: they wouldn't have had a nice home, nor balanced meals to eat, nor even the money to buy the razor my uncle was using to shave himself. Their lives would have been much worse.

Perhaps it's like the difference between the optimist and the pessimist. Let's say you were painting your house and realized you were on your last half-gallon of paint. Realizing this also made you realize it would not be enough to finish painting your house. You could take the attitude of an optimist and say "At least I still have half a gallon," or you could display the attitude of a pessimist by saying "I only have half a gallon left and will have to make another trip to the store." Looking for the good among the bad is very much this way. If we focus on all the bad in our lives we will soon not see any good, but if we find and focus on the good, the bad will move to the background of our lives.

Sonja, the boys, and I had to search for the good on many occasions. While the good was many times hidden by the bad, it was still there. There were times when we were covered up with continually mounting high medical bills, and many times were wondering how we would pay our bills or buy our groceries. When it seemed it couldn't become any worse, something would always happen which bailed us out. There was one time in particular which comes to mind. Sonja's sister, who lives out of state, wanted to come see Sonja before she died. Since she flew here, she had no car to drive and couldn't afford to rent one. Sonja gave her the keys to her car and told her to use it as long as she was here. Later on that week, my sister-in-law wrecked the car. Although your first thought is probably one of horror, this accident in actuality helped us. You see, about the time we were again out of money and worried about how we would pay for Sonja's next round of pain medications, a check for this now totaled car arrived, again bailing us out. While my sister-in-law felt bad about this accident, she in actuality came to our aid with this wreck. Thanks Janel, you were indeed a big help! As you can see, sometimes the good comes to us from unexpected sources. It has always been my opinion that God will take care of the ones who love him. Remember the verse I quoted earlier from Romans 8:28 – "...All things work together for good to them that love God... ." Indeed this verse may be taken to heart, for it never failed us, in our time of need.

When your needs are great and your resources low, there are always those who come through for you. Earlier I told you of the people I work with and how they had many fund raising events in our behalf. There was one time in which I literally had only fifty-eight dollars to my name, and again it was time to purchase more medications. At the time I was spending $1,391.00 every eight days on these drugs. With only fifty-eight dollars, you can imagine how worried I was. That day my fellow employees came through with the proceeds from a bake sale. This event raised more than enough to pay for the drugs. Again, there was no need to worry.

After Sonja's death, the worries changed somewhat even though they were still there, and these worries again brought about a hunt for the good among the bad. This time it was more of an emotional turmoil. Perhaps it was based upon the many questions we all had. Questions of how to do things which only Sonja had done in the past. Questions of "Dad, are you ever gonna get married again?" and of course my questions usually had to do with raising the kids without their mom. I was never a person who could easily express my emotions to my children. I had always held that as a feminine characteristic, therefore Sonja had always given them that kind of emotional support. I was usually the disciplinarian in the family. These, and many other things attributed to the bad in our lives, thus increasing our search for the good.

After some time, our grief began to let up, and by nature our eyes began to see more and more good. Our sometimes pessimistic ways began to shed, giving light to a new optimism. The emotional noose around our necks began to loosen, allowing us to breathe a little easier, and we again started to see the beauty of this magnificent world around us. We began to realize just how lucky we in actuality are. Lucky that the life insurance had paid everything off, lucky that we have all the friends we have, and lucky to have been able to spend the time we did with Sonja, making lasting memories. For these memories can help sustain us through the remainder of this life without her.

APPENDIX

55

For an excellent program designed to help your children overcome their grief, and better deal with their loss, <u>MAY I PERSONALLY RECOMMEND THE NATIONALLY KNOWN PROGRAM CALLED "RAINBOWS"</u>. For more information on this excellent program, contact:

RAINBOWS
1111 TOWER ROAD
SCHAUMBURG, IL 60173
(708) 310 - 1880

WHERE TO GO
FOR HELP

HELP FOR GRIEVING CHILDREN:

American Cancer Society
19 West 56th Street
New York, NY 10036
(212) 586-8700

Center for Living
704 Broadway, 3rd Floor
New York, NY 10003
(212) 533-3550

Center for Loss and Life Transition
3735 Broken Bow Road
Fort Collins, CO 80526
(303) 226-6050

Center for Sibling Loss
1700 W. Irving Park
Chicago, IL 60613
(312) 883-0268

Dougy Center
3909 S.E. 52nd
Portland, OR 97206
(503) 775-5683

Elisabeth Kubler - Ross Center
South Route 616
Headwaters, VA 24442
(703) 396-3441

Enrichment Groups Child and Family Services
1680 Albany Avenue
Hartford, CT 06105
(203) 236-4511

Grief Recovery Institute
8306 Wilshire Boulevard, Suite 21-A
Los Angeles, CA 90211
(800) 445-4808

Life With Cancer Program
Fairfax Program
3300 Gallows Road
Falls Church, VA 22046
(703) 698-2841

National Hospice Organization
1901 North Fort Myers Drive, Suite 902
Arlington, VA 22209
(703) 243-5900

The Good Grief Program
Judge Baker Guidance Center
295 Longwood Avenue
Boston, MA 02115
(617) 232-8390

HELP FOR THE GRIEVING ADULT:

Compassionate Friends
Box 1347
Oakbrook, IL 60521
(708) 990-0010

Hope for the Bereaved
1342 Lancaster Avenue
Syracuse, NY 13210
(315) 472-HOPE

National Hospice Organization
1901 North Fort Meyers Drive, Suite 902
Arlington, VA 22209
(703) 243-5900

National Self-Help Clearinghouse
25 W. 43rd Street, Room 620
New York, NY 10036
(212) 840-1259

THEOS Foundation
1301 Clark Building
717 Liberty Avenue
Pittsburgh, PA 15222
(412) 471-7779

Widowed Persons Services
A Program of AARP
1909 "K" Street N.W.
Washington, D.C. 20049
(202) 728-4370

Young Widows and Widowers, Ltd.
4 Whiffletree Circle
Andover, MA 01810
(508) 475-2857

OR CONTACT YOUR LOCAL CHAPTER OF:

–the United Way Information Service

–the local mental health agency

–the social service department of your local hospital

–a local church

–a local Hospice program

ORDER FORM

S.H.M. Publishing
P.O. Box 6089 - T
Abilene, TX 79608
Office / Fax: (915) 692 - 3223
SAN: 298 - 6442

Please send me_____copy/copies of the book **"When Death Is Imminent"** by Greg D. Hardegree, at the purchase price of $7.99 each plus shipping. (Texas residence add 8.25% for sales tax).

Price of book(s) $7.99 each...$_____

Texas residence sales tax (8.25%)...............................$_____

Shipping ($1.24 for the 1st book and 25¢ for each
additional copy...$_____

Enclosed is my check or money order for the total of.....$_____

Please ship it to:
(Print Clearly)

NAME:_____

ADDRESS:_____APT. #_____

CITY:_____STATE:_____ZIP:_____

PHONE (Optional):(____)_____-_____

There will be a $25.00 service charge on all returned checks.
Prices are subject to change without notice.
Please allow 4 - 6 weeks for delivery.

**<u>Look for these other books by Greg D. Hardegree,
due for release in 1996:</u>**

"The Many Faces of Grief"

"Emotionally Stressed – How to Deal With Stress From Grief"

☐ **Please put me on your mailing list so I will know when these
other books are available.**

7489